1

The need for
SPEED
Racing Cars

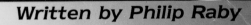

Written by Philip Raby

W
FRANKLIN WATTS
NEW YORK · LONDON · SYDNEY

This edition published in 2000 by Franklin Watts
96 Leonard Street
London EC2A 4XD

Franklin Watts Australia
14 Mars Road
Lane Cove
NSW 2066

© Franklin Watts 1999

Text: Philip Raby
Series editor: Matthew Parselle
Designed by: Perry Associates
Art director: Robert Walster

A CIP catalogue record for this book
is available from the British Library

ISBN 0 7496 3159 7 (Hb)
      0 7496 3918 0 (Pb)
Dewey Decimal Classification 796.7
Printed in Dubai

*Picture credits: Cover: Front top – Ford Motorsport;
front middle and back inset – Bryn Williams; front
bottom – National Motor Museum; back – Ford
Motorsport; Formula One – Ford Motorsport; Indycar –
Bryn Williams; LAT; Le Mans – LAT; Bryn Williams;
NASCAR – Allsport/Craig Jones/David Taylor/Jamie
Squire; Rally cars – Bryn Williams; Ford Motorsport;
LAT; Dragsters – Martin Grosse Geldermann; National
Motor Museum, Beaulieu; Supersonic – Allsport/David
Taylor; LAT; Baja 1000 – Allsport/Mike Powell; National
Motor Museum, Beaulieu; Allsport/Pascal Rondeau;
Camel Trophy – CGI Group; Bangers – Spedeworth
International Ltd; Dune buggies – Andy Bull; Karting –
Allsport/Mark Thompson; LAT; Vandystadt Agence de
Presse*

CONTENTS

4 – 5 **INTRODUCTION**

6 – 7 **FORMULA ONE**

8 – 9 **INDYCAR**

10 – 11 **LE MANS**

12 – 13 **NASCAR**

14 – 15 **RALLY CARS**

16 – 17 **DRAGSTERS**

18 – 19 **SUPERSONIC**

20 – 21 **BAJA 1000**

22 – 23 **CAMEL TROPHY**

24 – 25 **BANGERS**

26 – 27 **DUNE BUGGIES**

28 – 29 **KARTING**

30 **USEFUL CONTACTS**

31 **TECHNICAL TERMS**

32 **INDEX**

INTRODUCTION

If you've ever wanted to know what it feels like to drive some of the most powerful cars in the world then The Need for Speed will show you.

This book features the whole range of high-adrenaline motorsport experiences. Strap yourself into the cockpit of a Formula One car, watched by millions as you take part in the Grand Prix. Burn nitromethane in a top-fuel dragster as you disappear down the strip in a cloud of smoke. Feel the blistering acceleration of the record breaking Thrust SSC as you approach supersonic speeds.

As well as the thrills and spills, we also give you the facts and figures behind these incredible machines. For every type of car featured there is a Stat File and a Fact File.

The Stat File is a list of basic statistics about that type of car.

This line tells you the model of car used as an example. The model chosen will be one of the most powerful of that type of vehicle.

These lines give details about such things as engine size, acceleration and top speed. Some of the terms used are explained on page 31 of this book.

STAT FILE

Stewart-Ford SF-1

Engine type	Cosworth-Zetec
Engine size	2998cc
Power	730bhp
Number of cylinders	V10
Top speed	320km/h (200mph)
Acceleration	0-100km/h in 2.5 seconds

The Fact File gives a slightly unusual, strange or funny bit of information about the car.

FACT FILE

Grand Prix is French for Big Prize. Top Formula One drivers earn millions of pounds racing, but they have to be very fit to cope with driving such a small car at such high speeds for long periods. Drivers work out in the gym every day and many cycle long distances on mountain bikes to keep fit.

The Formula One Grand Prix is one of the most important race series of the year. The stakes are high, and the sport is watched on television by millions of people around the world.

Formula One cars are very small. The cockpit, which is in front of the powerful engine, is just big enough for the driver to fit into.

The engine drives the rear wheels, which are very wide to grip the track well. The front wheels are slightly smaller to make the car easy to steer at high speeds.

Modern Formula One cars are very complex. They use computers to check the engine's performance and send data back to the support crew in the pits. The cars do not have a gear-lever: instead, the driver changes gear by pressing buttons.

STAT FILE

Stewart-Ford SF-1

Engine type	Cosworth-Zetec
Engine size	2998cc
Power	730bhp
Number of cylinders	V10
Top speed	320km/h (200mph)
Acceleration	0-100km/h in 2.5 seconds

Sometimes Formula One cars crash. The cars are designed to protect the driver very well, so he is rarely badly injured. When there is a crash, the fuel from the car may explode, so drivers wear fireproof suits, gloves and boots.

Grand Prix is French for Big Prize. Top Formula One drivers earn millions of pounds racing, but they have to be very fit to cope with driving such a small car at such high speeds for long periods. Drivers work out in the gym every day and many cycle long distances on mountain bikes to keep fit.

In the pits

Formula One cars race at speeds of over 320km/h (200mph) about 60 times around the track. They have to stop at least once to refuel. They drive off the track into a pit lane. As soon as the car has stopped, a team of technicians starts work on the car. Not only do they put more fuel in, they may also change the tyres and wipe the driver's visor so that he can see clearly.

It is important that the car gets back into the race as quickly as possible, so the technicians work very fast. The car can be refuelled and fitted with new tyres in less than 20 seconds.

INDYCAR

Indycar racing is an American sport, which is similar to Formula One. The cars are less sophisticated but more powerful and just as exciting to watch. Indycar racing takes place in the United States, Canada and Australia. The cars are lightweight with very powerful engines, which means that they can travel at speeds of more than 380km/h (240mph).

Some Indycar races take place on oval tracks, which have two long straights and wide bends at each end. The bends are banked so that the cars can go around them without slowing down very much. At very high cornering speeds, the driver is flung outwards, so his head is held in place by removable polystyrene supports. Other races are held on more conventional tracks.

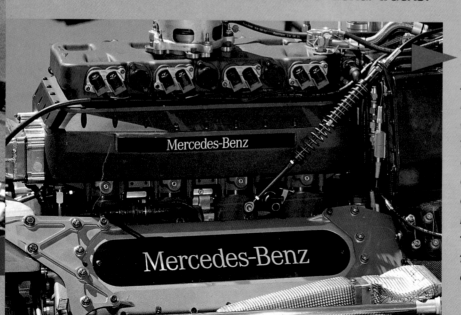

Mercedes-Benz

Mercedes-Benz

Most Indycars have turbocharged engines. A turbocharger is a big fan, driven by the exhaust gases, which forces fuel into the engine to give it lots of extra power. Some cars that drive on normal roads have turbochargers: look for the word 'Turbo' on the boot lid.

Tyres

Like many racing cars, Indycars can be fitted with different tyres to suit the weather. If the track is dry, the cars drive on smooth tyres called slicks. When it is raining, the driver will ask for tyres with grooves to be fitted. These help to stop the car sliding off the track. The tyres wear away very quickly and will only last for one race.

STAT FILE

Valvoline Reynard

Engine type	Honda turbocharged
Engine size	2600cc
Power	860bhp
Number of cylinders	V8
Top speed	380km/h (240mph)
Acceleration	0-100km/h in 2.5 seconds

FACT FILE

Indycar oval races always run in an anticlockwise direction. To help the cars go around corners better, the left rear tyre is very slightly smaller than the right-hand one.

LE MANS

Imagine driving a car for 24 hours – that's one whole day – non-stop. And at speeds of up to 400 km/h (250mph) too! There's a car race where drivers do exactly that: the Le Mans 24 hour.

Le Mans is normally a quiet French town, but in June every year it is besieged by thousands of people arriving to see one of the world's toughest and most exciting car races.

STAT FILE

Lister Storm GTL

Engine type	Lister petrol
Engine size	6996cc
Power	655bhp
Number of cylinders	V12
Top speed	400km/h (240mph)
Acceleration	0-100km/h in 2.2 seconds

Le Mans cars are specially built for the competition. They have to be very sturdy to survive being driven at high speed for such a long time. Some of the cars have their bodies built from a special material called carbon-fibre, which is light and very strong.

Many of the cars that start the race break down and don't finish. Le Mans is as much about durability as top speed. Unlike most races, Le Mans is not a fixed length: the winner is the car that completes the most laps in 24 hours.

Because the race runs overnight, the cars have very powerful headlights so that the drivers can see a long way ahead while travelling at speeds of over 320km/h (200mph).

It would be almost impossible for one person to drive so fast for the whole day, so the driving is shared between a team of two to three experienced racers.

FACT FILE

The first Le Mans 24-hour race was run in 1923. The winning car managed an average speed of 90 km/h (57mph): much less than the speeds of today's cars.

NASCAR

Nascar is a very popular type of motor racing in the USA. The initials stand for the National Association for Stock Car Racing. The cars travel at great speeds round and round an oval track, surrounded on both sides by concrete walls, with other cars battling to get past them.

NASCAR cars are based on normal saloon cars, but have much more powerful engines. They also need to be able to take a lot of abuse. Unlike most other types of racing, it is acceptable for NASCAR cars to collide.

The cars often bump into each other as they race together in tight clusters. At the end of the race, many of the cars will be badly dented. In fact, some cars get so badly damaged that they are unable to finish the race.

STAT FILE

Chevy Monte Carlo

Engine type	Chevrolet petrol
Engine size	5866cc
Power	700bhp
Number of cylinders	V8
Top speed	320km/h (200mph)
Acceleration	0-100km/h in under 3 seconds

NASCAR circuits

NASCAR races are held on special oval-shaped tracks. The corners slope inwards so that the cars can go around them at speeds nearing 320km/h (200mph). The cars always race in an anticlockwise direction.

The track is sometimes surrounded on both sides by a solid concrete wall to stop cars flying off. This is an added hazard for the drivers as they try to avoid being hit by other cars.

FACT FILE

Inside a NASCAR car there is a frame made from strong metal tubing. This is called a roll cage and helps to protect the driver in the event of an accident. Because there can be bits of car flying around during the race, even the windscreen may be protected by a metal grid.

RALLY CARS

Rally cars tear along dirt tracks, roads and cross-country at very high speeds. They skid around corners sideways, ripping up the ground and sending dust up into the air. One wrong move by the driver and the car can go flying off the track.

Rally cars are usually ordinary cars, which have been heavily modified for racing. The engine, wheels and suspension are made much stronger to cope with driving on rough, bumpy tracks.

The inside of a rally car looks very different to a normal car. There are no carpets; just a metal floor. And there is a roll cage made from steel tubes to make the car stronger and protect the people inside if the car rolls over. There are special seats and straps to hold the driver and passenger firmly in place as the car jolts along at 160km/h (100mph).

The passenger in a rally car is called a navigator or co-driver. His or her job is to read maps and directions provided by the race organiser, tell the driver which way to go and warn of bends, bumps and other hazards. Because the cars are so noisy, the driver and navigator talk to each other through microphones and headsets built into their helmets. If the navigator makes a mistake, valuable time could be wasted.

Rallies often continue through the night. The cars have a large bank of headlights at the front to help the driver and navigator see the way ahead.

STAT FILE

Subaru Impreza

Engine type	Subaru flat four
Engine size	1994cc
Power	300bhp
Number of cylinders	4
Top speed	190km/h (120mph)
Acceleration	0-100km/h in under 5 seconds

Rally Circuits

Most rallies are run on a mixture of roads and off-road tracks. The race is divided into sections called stages. When the cars are on public roads, they must drive carefully and not exceed the speed limits. But once they get off-road, they go as fast as they can.

Rally circuits are narrow, so the cars cannot overtake each other. Instead, cars start the race one after the other and are timed very carefully. The car that completes the circuit in the shortest time is the winner.

FACT FILE

In the 1960s, one of the most famous and successful rally cars was a souped-up version of the Mini called the Mini Cooper. Because Minis were small and light, they could drive very fast on winding tracks.

Dragsters are cars which are specially made to race at very high speeds in a straight line. The fastest dragsters can race at over 480km/h (300 mph).

Dragsters look unlike any other cars. They have huge wheels at the back with big tyres. Before the race starts, the driver spins the wheels to warm up the tyres. This makes them sticky so that they grip the track better. Spinning the wheels creates a big cloud of smoke behind the dragster.

Dragsters have extremely powerful engines. They are powered by a special fuel called nitromethane.

As the dragster accelerates down the track, the tiny front wheels lift off the ground. This is called a wheelie – just like you may do on your bicycle. Wheelies slow down the car, so dragsters have a bar at the back with little wheels on. This is called a wheelie bar and stops the car lifting up too high.

When the dragster has reached the end of its run it can be travelling at over 480km/h (300mph). The driver releases a parachute from the back of the car to help slow it down.

STAT FILE

Top-fuel Dragster

Engine type	Supercharged nitromethane
Engine size	8400cc
Power	6000bhp (for 4.5 secs only)
Number of cylinders	8
Top speed	520km/h (325mph)
Acceleration	0-480km/h in 5 seconds

Drag strip

Dragsters do not run on a circuit like most cars. Instead, they drive down a long straight track called a drag strip.

Drag strips are always 400m (1320ft) long. Some dragsters can complete the distance in under six seconds, which is very fast.

If the cars race in pairs along the drag strip, they are sometimes separated by a concrete wall for safety.

Wheelie Bar

FACT FILE

The rear wheels on a dragster spin so fast that the tyres noticeably increase in size because of the extreme forces.

SUPERSONIC

Not all racing cars are built to beat other cars. Some are built especially to break the land speed record. Ever since the car was first invented, people have been finding ways of going faster and faster. The latest record-breaking cars use massive jet engines to propel them at speeds of more than 1000km/h (600mph).

Travelling at such high speeds requires very long, straight, flat surfaces – over 20km (12 miles). Because of this, most record-breaking attempts are done in the USA on huge salt or sand flats.

The Thrust SuperSonic Car (SSC) was the first car to go supersonic. This means that it travelled at more than the speed of sound. Thrust SSC reached an incredible 1230km/h (764mph) in 1997.

FACT FILE

Thrust SSC was developed by a British company. It was driven by a British Royal Air Force officer who was used to travelling at high speeds in jet aircraft.

When a car or an aeroplane breaks the sound barrier – approximately 1200km/h (750mph) – it creates a very loud noise called a 'sonic boom'. When Thrust SSC went supersonic, the boom could be heard for miles around.

Normal tyres would break up at such speeds. Thrust SSC and its predecessor, Thrust II (below), had solid metal wheels with no tyres.

Deserts are hot, dry and dusty: not the ideal place for a car race. But people do race in deserts. Because of the tough conditions and the long distances involved, the rallies aren't just about speed – they're also about completing the race in one piece.

One of the most famous desert races is the Baja 1000. Baja (say ba-ha) is an area in northern Mexico. A lot of it is desert. Every year hundreds of cars (and trucks and motorcycles) head into the desert for the Baja 1000 race. As the name would suggest, the course is about 1000 miles (1600km) long.

All car engines need to suck in air to operate. In a desert, the engine could suck in sand as well and be damaged. To avoid this,

Air Intake

some desert rally cars have huge air intakes high up on the roof, as far away from the sand as possible. This car is taking part in the Paris-Dakar rally between Paris in France and Dakar in North Africa.

All sorts of vehicles enter the race. The most successful ones are specially made desert rally cars. These are based on ordinary family saloons, but are raised up on big wheels so that they can drive over rough ground.

STAT FILE

Desert Rally Car

Engine Type	V-12
Engine Size	6064cc
Number of Cylinders	12
Power	600bhp
Top Speed	320km/h (200mph)
Acceleration	0-100km/h in 2.2 seconds

FACT FILE

Although deserts are hot during the day, they become very cold at night. The combination of cold and hot makes desert rallies very uncomfortable for the competitors and increases the risk of the cars breaking down.

Well equipped

Unlike other types of motor racing, desert rally cars cannot drive into the pits for refuelling or repairs. Instead, the cars have an extra large tank to carry all the fuel they need to cover the long race.

It can get very hot in the desert, so the cars are packed with containers of water for both the engine and for the drivers to drink.

If the car breaks down, the driver and co-driver have to be able to repair it. They carry spare parts and tools to help them do this.

CAMEL TROPHY

Most vehicles are designed to drive on roads or race tracks. Some, though, are made especially to go 'off-road' on grass and mud. The most famous off-roaders are Land Rovers. Every year Land Rovers compete in the world's greatest adventure: the Camel Trophy.

The Camel Trophy is held in a different part of the world every year. It is always a wild, unexplored area that tests the vehicles and the drivers to their limits.

All the vehicles that take part are either Land Rover Freelanders or Discoveries, similar to the ones you see driving on the road. The vehicles are identical, which means that winning the Camel Trophy event is down to the skill of the teams.

Four wheel drive

Most cars are built so that the engine turns just two wheels: either the front ones or the back ones. Land Rovers are four-wheel-drive vehicles. This means that the engine turns all four wheels. Four wheel drive makes the vehicle grip much better on slippery surfaces such as mud. You may also hear a four-wheel-drive vehicle called a four by four or 4x4.

Some Land Rovers have two gear-levers. One is for changing gear, just like you'll see in a normal car. The second is to set the gearbox to high ratio or low ratio. Low ratio is used for driving very slowly up and down steep hills.

Land Rover Freelander

Engine type	Rover diesel
Engine size	1900cc
Number of cylinders	4
Power	72bhp
Top speed	154km/h (96mph)
Acceleration	0-100km/h in 14.6 seconds

Most car races are won by the fastest car. But the Camel Trophy is not just about speed. The winning team is the one that most successfully negotiates the many obstacles over the journey. At times, the vehicles may only be travelling at 8km/h (5mph) up and down hills or through rivers, mud, snow and ice.

On the front of each vehicle is a drum with a wire rope around it. This is called a winch. If the Land Rover gets stuck, the team get out, unwind the wire and attach it to a strong tree or rock. The winch has a motor, which winds up the wire and slowly pulls the vehicle free.

FACT FILE

The first Camel Trophy was run in 1980 using American Jeep four-wheel-drive vehicles. Later events have used British Land Rovers.

BANGERS

What do you think happens to road cars when they reach the end of their lives? Most go to scrapyards where they are broken up. Some, through, go out with a real bang.

Banger racing is one of the cheapest forms of motorsport to get into. All you need is an old car and a crash helmet.

STAT FILE

Ford Granada Banger

Engine type	Ford petrol
Engine size	2933cc
Number of cylinders	V6
Power	150bhp
Top speed	215km/h (135mph)
Acceleration	0-100km/h in 10 seconds

The old cars are completely stripped of seats, carpets and glass to make them lighter and to reduce the risk of bits flying off during the race. The doors, bonnet and boot are welded up so that they cannot be opened – the driver has to climb in though the window.

Banger racing is a lot of fun to watch. Many of the cars are not very fast, so the drivers try to win the race by smashing into other cars to get them off the track. By the end of the race, the cars are completely bashed up and fit only for the scrapyard!

Different types of car

Some cars are faster than others, so to make banger racing fair, there are different classes of racing for different engine sizes. There are even banger races for ice cream vans, cars towing caravans, classic cars and three-wheel cars!

FACT FILE

In Europe, stock car racing uses specially made cars in a more advanced type of banger racing. Stock cars are made from strong metal bars so they can smash into each other without being damaged. Don't confuse these cars with the very different American stock cars
(see pages 12-13)

25

DUNE BUGGIES

A lot of people enjoy racing small, stripped-down cars called buggies. The races take place on off-road tracks: either along sand dunes on beaches or in deserts, or on dirt tracks in the countryside. It's a fun hobby and it's also fairly cheap to get into; most of the vehicles are home-made using an engine and other parts from the popular Volkswagen Beetle car.

Just like the Beetle, buggies have their engine in the back, where it is connected to the big rear wheels. The front of the car has much smaller wheels to make the car easy to steer. Most racing cars have very wide tyres to grip the track, but buggies have narrower tyres, which are better for driving on loose surfaces.

Buggies race up and down hills and dunes, which can have steep sides. Sometimes the buggies roll over, but the drivers are firmly strapped in and there are strong metal frames for protection, so it is unlikely that they will be injured. Usually, when a buggy rolls over, three or four people can turn it the right way up again so that the driver can continue racing. Some buggies have handles along the sides to make it easier to lift.

VW Beetle Buggy

Engine type	Tuned flat-four petrol
Engine size	1600cc
Power	60bhp or more
Number of cylinders	4
Top speed	160km/h (100mph)
Acceleration	0-100km/h in 8 seconds

Air-cooled engines

Car engines get hot when they are running. If they are not kept cool, they will overheat and blow up. Most engines are cooled by water, but the Volkswagen Beetle engines used in buggies are different; they are cooled with air.

An air-cooled engine is ideal for a buggy because there is no water to leak out if the engine is damaged.

FACT FILE

The Volkswagen Beetle, on which most dune buggies are based, was first built more than 50 years ago.

KARTING

There's a type of motor sport that both children and adults can compete in. It's called karting and is one of the most popular forms of motor racing.

Karts are tiny little racing cars that you sit on rather than in. They only have a very small engine similar to a motorcycle engine – but because karts are so light, they can still accelerate quickly up to around 110km/h (70mph). This seems especially fast when you are sitting so close to the ground!

Karts have tiny wheels with smooth tyres. These allow them to slide round corners just like a real racing car.

There are over 20 classes of kart racing in the UK. Junior classes include races for 8 to 12 year olds and 12 to 16 year olds. Senior classes are for anyone over 16 years old.

The classes are subdivided according to the engine power and gearbox type.

STAT FILE

Honda GXS160 Pro

Engine type	Honda 4-stroke
Engine size	160cc
Power	12bhp
Number of cylinders	V10
Top speed	120km/h (75mph)
Acceleration	0-100km/h in 6 seconds

Getting into motor racing

Many top racing drivers started off in karting: it's a good way to learn the skills needed to drive fast around a circuit.

If you dream of being a racing driver, you should consider getting started in karting. Although it is expensive to buy a kart and all the necessary equipment, many towns have indoor fun-kart tracks where you can have a go driving a kart. These karts do not go as fast as racing ones: they have a top speed of around 65km/h (40mph), but are still great fun to drive. They do not have gears, so they're easier for beginners to control.

FACT FILE

Karting was invented in the 1950s by an American called Art Ingals. Back then it was called go-karting. The very first karts were made from drainpipes and lawnmower engines.

USEFUL CONTACTS

If you want to get involved in some of the motor sports mentioned in this book, either to watch or to actually take part, here are some names and numbers that might be useful.

UK

British Racing Drivers' Club Limited
Silverstone Towcester
Northamptonshire NN12 8TN
Tel: 01327 857271
Fax: 01327 858276
The club for racing drivers of all types

British Stock Car Association
Long Eaton Stadium Long Eaton
Nottinghamshire
Tel: 0181 360 7978
The controlling body for stock car racing

RAC Motor Sports Association Limited
Motor Sports House Riverside Park
Colnbrook Slough SL3 0HG
Tel: 01753 681736
Fax: 01753 682938
The national body controlling most forms of motor sport

National Kart Racing Association
50 Newton Road Dalton-in-Furness
Cumbria LA15 8NF
Tel: 01229 463748
For all you need to know about karting

Silverstone Circuits Limited
Silverstone Towcester
Northamptonshire NN12 8TN
Tel: 01327 311164
Fax: 01327 857663
The home of Formula One racing in the UK also hosts other events, including rally stages

Santa Pod Raceway Airfield Road
Hinwick Northamptonshire NN29 7JQ
Tel: 01234 782828
Fax: 01234 782818
The home of drag racing in the UK

Spedeworth International Ltd
2 Faraday Court Rankine Road
Basingstoke Hampshire RG24 8PF
Tel: 01256 333277
Fax: 01256 333288
Organisers of short circuit racing – including banger and stock car racing

AUSTRALIA

Eastern Creek Raceway
Australian Racing Driver Club Ltd
Horsley Road Eastern Creek
Eastern Creek 2148

There are some words in this book which you may not have seen before. Here is an explanation of them.

Accelerate: drive faster.

Air intakes: holes in a car, which let air into the engine. The engine needs air to run and to keep it cool.

Bonnet: a lifting panel, usually at the front of a car, that covers the engine compartment.

Boot: a compartment at the rear of a car that holds luggage.

Brakes: a mechanism inside a car's wheels that makes it stop when the driver presses a pedal.

Brake horsepower: see horsepower.

CC: short for cubic capacity, the measure of an engine's size. Usually, the greater the cc of an engine, the more powerful it is.

Circuit: a track that racing cars drive around.

Cylinders: parts inside an engine where the fuel burns. Most cars have four cylinders, but more powerful engines may have six, eight or even twelve cylinders.

Durability: how well a car will last and cope with rough treatment.

Engine: a machine inside a car, which turns the wheels and makes the car move.

Four wheel drive: a system where the engine turns all four wheels for better grip.

Fuel: liquid that burns inside the engine to make it run. Most cars run on either petrol or diesel fuel.

Gears: these allow a car to drive fast without the engine running too fast. Most cars have five gears. The gears may be selected by the driver or automatically by the car.

Gear-lever: a control inside a car, which the driver uses to change gear as the car moves faster or slower.

Horsepower: a measure of an engine's power. The higher the horsepower, the faster the car. Most family car engines are about 100 horsepower. A fast sports car may have a 300-horsepower engine, whereas many top-fuel dragsters are 6500 horsepower! You may see horsepower written as bhp, which stands for brake horsepower.

Jet engine: a type of engine that pushes hot gases out of the back of the car to make it move along. Jet engines are only used in special record-breaking cars, such as Thrust SSC.

Kilometers per hour (km/h): speed is measured by the number of kilometers a car will travel in one hour. For instance, at 30km/h the car will travel 30 kilometers in one hour. Speed can also be measured in miles per hour (mph).

Off-roader: a vehicle that can be driven on rough ground

Pit lane: an area at the side of a race track where cars go to be refuelled, have their tyres changed, and be repaired.

Roll cage: strong steel bars inside a car to protect the driver and any passengers in case of an accident.

Saloon: a four- or five-seater family car with a separate boot space and two or four doors.

Suspension: springs to which a car's wheels are attached to help it ride over bumps smoothly.

Tyres: rubber rings full of air that surround the wheels. Tyres allow the car to drive smoothly and quietly and help it to grip the road.

Turbocharger: a pump driven by exhaust gases, which forces air and fuel into the engine to increase the power.

Visor: a sun shade on a driver's helmet.

Windscreen: a large glass window at the front of the car, which the driver and passenger look through. It protects the occupants from wind, rain and cold.

INDEX

aircraft 18, 19
America 23, 28; see also USA
Australia 8

Baja 1000 20-21
bangers 24-25
buggies 26-27

Camel Trophy 22-23
carbon-fibre 10
Chevy Monte Carlo 12
clothing for drivers 6, 14, 24
cockpit 6
co-driver 14, 21
computers 6
cornering 8, 9, 13, 14, 28
crashes 6, 24, 25

desert rally cars 20-21
dragsters 16-17
drag strip 17
drivers 6, 8, 11, 13, 14, 16, 21, 22,
    24, 26
dune buggies 26-27

engines 6, 8, 14, 16, 18, 20, 22,
    25, 26, 27, 28, 29
    turbocharged 8
    see also Stat Files
exhaust 8

Ford Granada Banger 24
Formula One 6-7, 8
four wheel drive 22, 23
fuel 6, 7, 8, 16, 21
    tanks 21

gearboxes 28
gears 6, 22, 29
Grand Prix 6-7

headlights 11, 14
Honda GXS160 Pro 28

Indycar racing 8-9

Jeep 23

karting 28-29

Land Rover 22
    Discoveries 22
    Freelanders 22, 23
Le Mans 24 hour race 10-11
Lister Storm GTL 10

Mini Cooper 15

NASCAR (National Association for
    Stock Car Racing) 12-13
navigator 14
nitromethane 16

parachute 16
Paris-Dakar rally 20
passengers 14
pit 6, 21

race tracks 7, 8, 9, 12, 13, 14, 15,
    17, 22
rally cars 14-15
refuelling 7, 21
roll cage 13, 14

speed 6, 7, 8, 10, 11, 12, 13, 14,
    16, 17, 18, 19, 23, 28, 29
    limits 15
    records 18
    see also Stat Files
steering 6, 26
Stewart-Ford SF-1 6
stock car racing 25
Subaru Impreza 15
suspension 14

Thrust SSC 18-19
Top-fuel Dragster 17
turbocharger 8
tyres 7, 9, 16, 17, 19, 26, 28

USA 8, 12, 18; see also America

Valvoline Reynard 9
VW Beetle 26, 27

wheelie 16

wheels 6, 14, 16, 17, 19, 20,
    26, 28